This book belongs to:

_____

T0035963

To my parents, thank you for always being interested. And for Elodie, always.

— Zoë

To N, my favourite person to talk to, because family is found.

— Anja

First edition published in 2023 by Flying Eye Books Ltd.
27 Westgate Street, London, E8 3RL.

Text © Zoë Armstrong
Illustrations © Anja Sušanj

Expert consultant: Dr Laura Kelley

Zoë Armstrong and Anja Sušanj have asserted their rights under the Copyright, Designs and Patents Act, 1988, to be identified as the Author and Illustrator of this Work.

All rights reserved. No part of this publication may be reproduced or transmitted in any form or by any means, electronic or mechanical, including photocopying, recording or by any information and storage retrieval system, without prior written consent from the publisher.

Every attempt has been made to ensure any statements written as fact have been checked to the best of our abilities. However, we are still human, thankfully, and occasionally little mistakes may crop up. Should you spot any errors, please email info@nobrow.net.

1 3 5 7 9 10 8 6 4 2

Edited by Sara Forster
Designed by Lilly Gottwald

Published in the US by Flying Eye Books Ltd.
Printed in China on FSC® certified paper.

ISBN: 978-1-83874-035-1
www.flyingeyebooks.com

Zoë Armstrong   Anja Sušanj

Curious Creatures
TALKING
TOGETHER

Flying Eye Books

There's a lot of chatter here on Earth. The planet hums and pings and buzzes with talk, as we make connections and swap messages with our friends.

Messages that we send with words, and messages that we send in other ways...

Like waving a hand,

ringing a bell

or wearing special clothes.

But did you know that all around us animals are 'talking' together too, in all sorts of wordless ways. They signal with sounds and smells and curious movements. And when we learn to read the signals, we discover what these amazing creatures might actually be saying...

It is a misty morning in the Scottish Highlands.
These young hikers watch as a red deer stag roars
and bellows and stamps his hooves.

*Physical fights tend to happen when two similar
size stags can't tell from their communication
signals which is the strongest.*

The Red Deer

The two stags are in competition. They are using body language
and noisy roars to decide which of them is the biggest, strongest
and most powerful beast.

If neither stag backs down, they will raise their heads and walk
alongside each other, showing off their muscles and the size
of their antlers, working out which one would likely win a fight.
It's called *parallel walking*.

Stags send out these signals during the mating season when
they are competing for female deer. This kind of communication
has evolved to avoid a physical battle. The smaller stag will
often run off before any serious damage is done.

Another stag is nearby. He dips his head and thrashes the ground, tearing out the long grass with his mighty antlers, decorating them like a crown.

A stag will thrash the ground to intimidate his rival. The tangle of twigs and grass in his antlers might make him look bigger and more fearsome.

JUST LIKE YOU

Like the stags, perhaps you communicate to sort out disagreements without fighting. But instead of being fearsome, you might talk and listen and shake hands to make peace.

What is Animal Communication?

When an animal sends out a signal, which prompts another animal to change its behaviour, we say they are *communicating*. Communication helps with important things, like finding food, attracting a mate, avoiding danger or working together as a group. Only humans can actually speak, though – the brains of other creatures aren't complex enough for this – but they 'talk' in all kinds of amazing ways...

Many animals communicate with visual signals – signals that can be seen. These creatures are using body language to get their messages across...

A **raven** in the Northern Alps is pointing out handy objects to her friend. 'Look at this,' she seems to say. She points with her beak and wings, just as we humans use our hands to make gestures. This is very unusual in the animal kingdom.

Facial expressions can communicate how we are feeling. Apes and monkeys show emotions on their faces too. This young **gorilla** in Angola is saying, 'I want to play!' Her relaxed 'play face' has an open mouth and low hanging bottom lip, with no teeth on display.

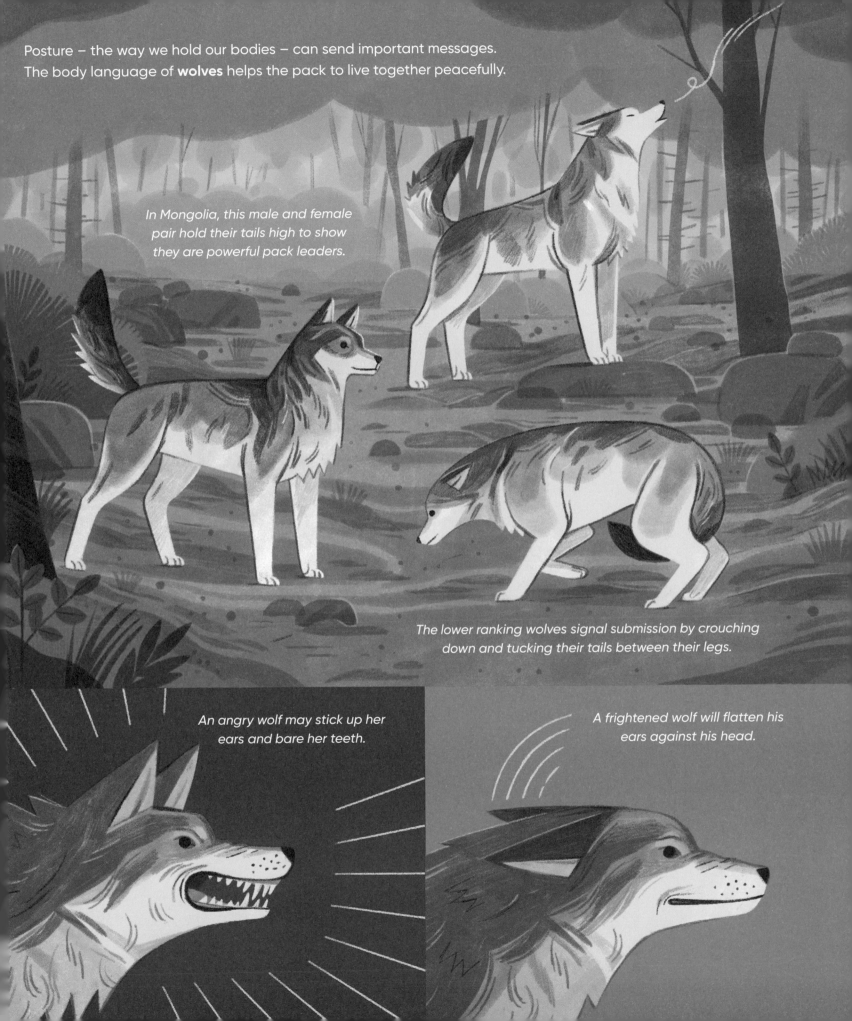

Posture – the way we hold our bodies – can send important messages.
The body language of **wolves** helps the pack to live together peacefully.

In Mongolia, this male and female pair hold their tails high to show they are powerful pack leaders.

The lower ranking wolves signal submission by crouching down and tucking their tails between their legs.

An angry wolf may stick up her ears and bare her teeth.

A frightened wolf will flatten his ears against his head.

In Australia, a biologist peers through the long lens of his camera, as a tiny creature - no bigger than a grain of rice - performs a mesmerising dance.

It waves for attention, then unfurls two dazzling flaps from around its vibrating body, like a fan. It sidesteps and scuttles and shimmies and shakes a pair of white-tipped legs in the air.

The Peacock Spider

This nifty mover is a peacock spider. With his colourful dance he is sending out communication signals to an earthy-coloured female. She is carefully watching his courtship display with her eight eyes.

His routine becomes more and more vigorous as he zig-zags towards her, flapping his fan and letting loose with his legs. 'See how healthy and energetic I am,' he seems to say. His markings look like the face of a wasp – perhaps the sight of a possible predator makes the female freeze and pay close attention. If she isn't enchanted by the male spider's mating message, she may pounce and eat him!

Biologist and photographer, Jurgen Otto, spends his life filming and discovering new species of peacock spider. His amazing videos are all over the internet!

The vibrations that peacock spiders make with their bodies when they dance are known as 'rumble rumps', 'crunch rolls' and 'grind-revs'.

JUST LIKE YOU

When you really want to be noticed, colourful clothes and fancy dance moves might be your favourite mode of communication too!

Vibrant Visual Signals

Some creatures 'talk' with dazzling displays of colour and movement and light. These *visual signals* are amazing adverts for animals seeking a mate...

The Satin Bowerbird

These satin bowerbirds, in Australia, have a thing for the colour blue. The male, with his indigo sheen, builds a stick structure called a bower.

He decorates the bower with a collection of bright blue objects that he finds. Flowers and shells, bottle tops, clothes pegs and drinking straws. He paints the walls with saliva and chewed plants.

When the olive-green female shows up, the male struts and bows and flicks his wings. He holds something blue in his beak – it matches the colour of his eyes. He makes all kinds of buzzing and hissing and whistling sounds. 'Look how blue I am,' he seems to say. 'I'm very attractive and blue'.

The Flamboyant Cuttlefish

Most of the time this flamboyant cuttlefish, in Indonesia, is camouflaged against the shallow seabed. But his skin contains special pigment cells, called *chromatophores*, which can change colour in a flash! The colours move in ripples across his body as he puts on a kaleidoscopic display. His eye-catching signals are used to attract a female cuttlefish, and sometimes to communicate aggression and startle a predator.

The Ostracods

In the western Caribbean Sea there are ostracods – tiny shrimp-like creatures – that communicate with twinkling patterns of glowing mucus. As night falls, the male ostracods dance up through the water column, leaving blobs of *bioluminescence*, like fairy lights, for the females to follow. A dazzling way to message a mate!

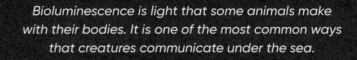

Bioluminescence is light that some animals make with their bodies. It is one of the most common ways that creatures communicate under the sea.

'Rraup! Rraup!' cries a vervet monkey in Kenya.
She has spotted danger: there's an eagle circling overhead!

All the other monkeys in the troupe glance skywards
at the sound of her low-pitched call. Then they leap
into bushes for cover, or scamper down branches to hide
deeper within the trees, safe from the bird of prey.

The Vervet Monkey

In the 1970s two scientist – Dorothy Cheney and her husband Robert
Seyfarth – showed that vervet monkeys have different cries to warn
their friends about different kinds of predators. They hid loudspeakers
in bushes, near groups of vervets in Kenya, and played recordings of
the monkeys' alarm calls. The sounds made the monkeys spring into
action, even when no predators were around.

They discovered that these were clear signals, not just yelps of fear.
The alarm calls are more like words, communicating information
about a particular danger, each with its own escape plan.

A low-pitched rraup sound means EAGLE! The monkeys look up at the sky then dive into bushes.

RRAUP!

A barking sound signifies, LEOPARD! The monkeys dash for the tips of tree branches, where big cats cannot reach them.

BARK!

A high-pitched chutter means SNAKE! The monkeys rear up on their legs, scanning the ground for pythons.

JUST LIKE YOU

You might yell, 'CAR' if a friend hasn't spotted danger while crossing the road, or 'BALL' if your ball might bop someone.

17

Extraordinary Sound Signals

Sound signals are an important way that animals 'talk' to each other. Non-human creatures can't speak, but many of them cry and roar and bark and squeak, and pretty much everything in between! Some animals communicate with sound in quite extraordinary ways...

There are big sounds that travel great distances...

The roar of the **lion** is the loudest of all the big cats. Its deep, gravelly rumblings can be heard up to eight kilometres away, across the plains of Africa. The square shape of their super-strong vocal cords allows lions to make a BIG noise.

Lions roar to keep in touch with friends and intimidate their rivals. 'I'm here and I'm POWERFUL,' the roar says.

Small sounds that are totally unique...

Brazilian free-tailed bat mothers leave their pups in huge cave crèches while they fly off to forage at night. When a mother returns, she must find her own pup amongst thousands of bat babies huddled together in the crèche.

Each pup has a unique cry. They call out as if to say, 'Over here, Mumma!' The mother bat can pick out the sound of her baby from the crowd, then she uses her sense of smell to be extra sure.

And teeny-tiny sounds that communicate with other species...

Some butterflies have an extraordinary relationship with ants. In Southern England and parts of Europe, the caterpillars and pupae of the **chalkhill blue** are guarded by ants, and communicate with them by 'singing'!

Ants feed on a sugary substance made by the caterpillars, and in return they offer protection from wasps and other insect predators. The caterpillars and pupae call out to the ants with tiny chirping sounds, as if to say, 'Here I am!'

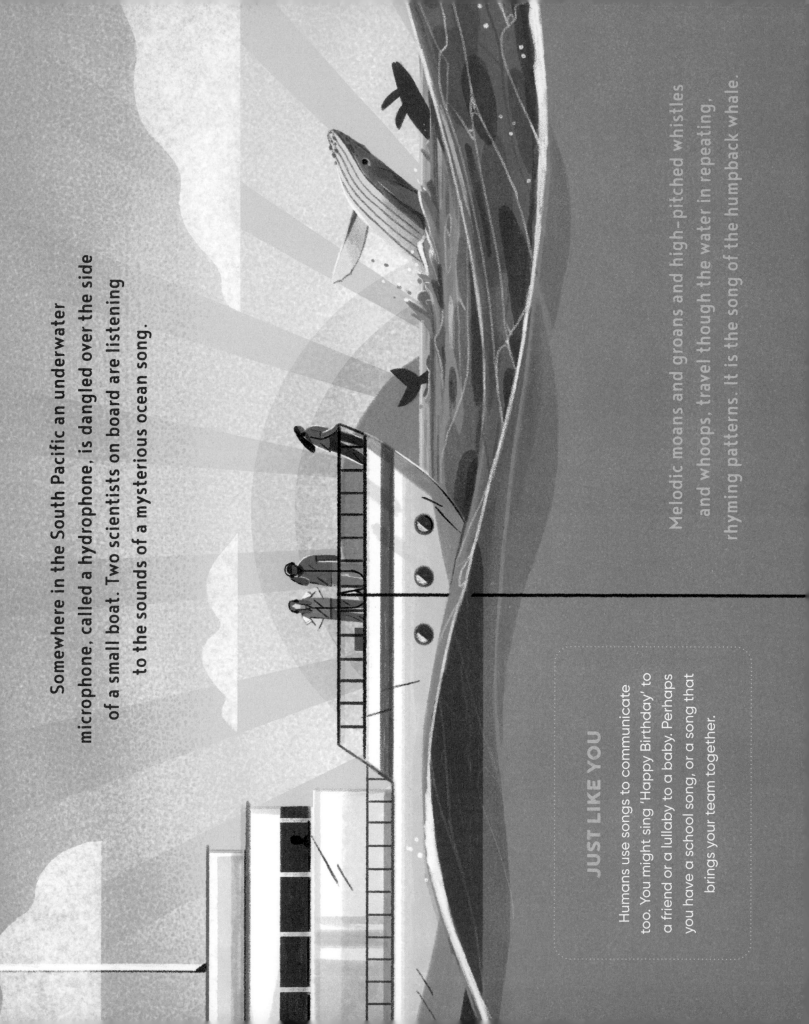

Somewhere in the South Pacific an underwater microphone, called a hydrophone, is dangled over the side of a small boat. Two scientists on board are listening to the sounds of a mysterious ocean song.

Melodic moans and groans and high-pitched whistles and whoops, travel though the water in repeating, rhyming patterns. It is the song of the humpback whale.

JUST LIKE YOU

Humans use songs to communicate too. You might sing 'Happy Birthday' to a friend or a lullaby to a baby. Perhaps you have a school song, or a song that brings your team together.

Males will sing for hours on end, reaching out to other humpbacks across many kilometres. Their song is probably a way to attract a mate or to compete with other males.

The Humpback whale

Humpback whales all over the planet have been communicating with sound for millions of years. The males make songs by arranging different noises into complex patterns – a bit like how human songs have verses, a chorus and maybe a guitar solo!

All the males in a particular part of the ocean sing the same song. But whales like novelty, and they make small changes over the years. Eventually a new shared song evolves.

In the Southern Pacific, dramatic 'song revolutions' take place! Every so often, all the humpbacks across a huge area suddenly scrap their old song, and replace it with an exciting new one, learned from a neighbouring whale population. Scientists think this happens because southern whales rarely meet other groups – when they do, they learn fast!

Playing Special Sounds

Whales and songbirds and some types of frog are known for their singing. But some curious creatures communicate with sound as if playing a musical instrument...

The **lowland streaked tenrec** of eastern Madagascar uses special quills on its back to play a chirping sound. It rubs the quills together like a violinist moving a bow across the strings of her instrument.

The high-pitched chirps can't always be picked up by human ears, but the sound may help tenrecs to find each other in the undergrowth. 'We're over here,' they seem to say.

Tenrecs are the only mammals known to communicate in this way. Crickets, and some other insects and snakes, are well known for rubbing body parts together to make a sound. It's called *stridulation*.

Male **palm cockatoos** in north-eastern Australia make a tool to use as a drumstick. This huge parrot breaks off a branch and strips away the bark. He will then grasp the stick in his left foot (it's almost always the left!) and begin to drum rhythmically on the side of a tree hollow.

Most of the drumming seems to happen near the nest, when the bird wants to impress a female. He will add a screech here, a whistle there, and flourish his extraordinary crest. If the female is impressed, she will come over to inspect the nest, checking it is good enough for a future chick.

It is a spring day in France, and these people are enjoying a picnic in the park. They are joined by a tiny curious creature, then another and another...

Within minutes, hundreds of hungry ants are marching in an organised line towards a sticky cake. The ants have a clever way of communicating where to find the food!

Ants spend a lot of time cleaning their antennae so they are primed to detect important smells.

The Ants

Ants use special smells called pheromones to 'talk' to each other. When a worker ant is out foraging, she leaves a pheromone trail for other ants to follow. If she finds food, she will make the trail stronger by leaving more of the scent on her way back to the nest.

Other ants pick up these smelly chemical signals with their antennae. They follow the scent trail all the way from the nest to the food source, each one laying down more pheromone as they go, making the trail stronger and stronger. Like a well organised army, thousands of ants are soon marching towards the food.

Some ant species also communicate with sound. They make chirping noises by rubbing together parts of their abdomen when they are in danger or to communicate where the best food is.

JUST LIKE YOU

Who hasn't been tempted to the table by the whiff of a good meal! But humans communicate with smells in other ways too. Scientists have found we can sense when people are anxious by the way they smell.

Ants release an alarm pheromone to warn of danger. Pheromones also allow ants to detect the social status of other ants and learn which ones belong to rival colonies.

Speaking With Smelly Signals

Smell is one of the most common ways that creatures pick up information. Foxes, for example, scent-mark their territory with the pungent pong of pee and poop. These smelly messages let other foxes know that an area is taken, and probably help to prevent fights.

In Madagascar, male **ring-tailed lemurs** take this a step further with aggressive stink fights! These primates secrete smelly chemicals from scent glands on their wrists and chests, as well as near their bottoms. They rub these smells over their long tails and waft them at their rivals.

Both male and female ring-tailed lemurs get themselves into some pretty peculiar positions as they scent mark their territories!

The smells map out the lemurs' living spaces, communicate information about social status, and help them to attract a mate.

Pheromones

Pheromones are smells that have evolved to trigger a particular reaction in animals of the same species. All pheromones are smells, but not all smells are pheromones.

The lives of social insects, such as ants and bees, are ruled by these smelly signals. Pheromones may warn of danger, give directions and set off all kinds of complex behaviours.

Female moths release a pheromone into the night air to attract a mate. The scent is carried by the breeze and can be picked up by the antennae of a male moth several kilometres away. He flutters towards the female, following the scent in a zig-zag pattern, from air pocket to air pocket, until he finds her.

There are only tiny differences between the pheromones of closely related moth species, but moths know exactly which scent to follow.

In Botswana, these young conservationists gaze at a herd of elephants as they amble through the long grass.

A mother elephant gently touches her calf with her trunk as they walk. The calf is tired and he pushes his body against her front legs as if to say, 'Let's stop for a while, Mumma'.

The Elephants

The elephants are 'talking' using touch. This is an important way of communicating and bonding in elephant societies. The sensitive tips of their long trunks are used to stroke and comfort and explore each other.

Groups of elephants passing each other in the wilderness will often stop to exchange touches. This also helps them to learn about each other by sniffing out smells and chemical signals.

Scientists think that touch might even help elephants to pick up warning signals from many kilometres away. Soft pads on the soles of their feet let them sense vibrations in the earth's surface. They can actually feel the distant foot-stomping and low-pitched rumbling sounds made by a faraway herd in danger.

Communicating with touch is probably something you do every day. Maybe you hug someone goodbye as you go off to school or high-five your friends when you see them.

Just as humans hug, elephants entwine their trunks as a sign of affection.

29

Touching Messages

Lots of creatures use touch as way of 'talking' together – we call this tactile communication. Animals may have skin which is rich in sensory nerves, antennae that touch and tap, or feet that feel for vibrations...

The Termites

Termites and ants send tactile signals with their antennae. These termites in China are *tandem running*. One insect follows the other by tapping the leader's back legs. 'I'm right here,' it seems to say. If the termite at the back stops tapping, the leader turns around to find it.

The Polar Bear

Polar bears often communicate with their noses and paws. In Greenland, this bear is asking to share another bear's meal by touching her nose with his own.

Mother polar bears use their snouts and paws to nuzzle and send comforting signals to their cubs. Sometimes they will scold a little bear with a soft swipe of the paw.

The Walrus

During the breeding season, male walruses use their huge bodies to scare away other males. This walrus in Alaska is using headbutts and flipper-slaps to say, 'I'm more powerful than you, so go away!'

The Barbary Macaque

Apes and monkeys groom one another as a way of saying, 'Hey, I'm your friend'. In the Atlas Mountains in Morocco, these Barbary macaques are bonding through touch. Scientists have found that grooming their pals helps these macaques to relax and cooperate with each other.

At a wildlife sanctuary in Australia, a kangaroo is making puppy dog eyes at a human researcher. He really wants a snack.

The snacks are stuck inside a box, which the kangaroo can't open. He gazes at the human, then at the box, then back at the human again.

He hops over and nudges the human with his nose. He paws at his knee: 'Open the box,' he seems to say, 'I'm peckish'.

The Kangaroo

Researchers in Australia have discovered that kangaroos communicate with humans using body language, in the same way that dogs and horses do. This was a surprise because kangaroos have never been *domesticated* – they have never been bred to live alongside people.

The researchers worked with kangaroos living in sanctuaries and wildlife parks. They put pieces of sweet potato, carrot and corn into a box that was impossible for the kangaroos to open – then they watched what happened.

The kangaroos turned to a nearby human for help. It seems that even wild animals can sometimes learn to communicate with people just by being around them!

JUST LIKE YOU

If you have a pet dog or cat, you will be used to 'talking' with animals. Maybe your cat meows for food, or your dog sits when you tell him to.

The kangaroos are communicating with humans through 'gaze'. Goats, dogs and horses do this too – they will intentionally turn to stare at a person when they want help solving a problem.

33

Talking With Humans

Some animals have been bred, over thousands of years, to live or work alongside people. Cats, dogs, horses and goats have adapted to human life. They are *domesticated*, and have special ways of 'talking' with us.

The Dog

Dogs raise the inner part of their eyebrows, and show their tongues, much more often when a human is looking. Scientists think that 'puppy dog eyes' and other canine facial expressions really are a way of trying to communicate with us.

A dog's tail can send signals about how they are feeling. Italian scientists have found that happy dogs wag their tails more to their right, but dogs that are feeling nervous will wag towards the left. This is probably linked to how the two sides of the brain process emotions.

The Cat

They *yowl* and *growl*, *hiss* and *purr*, but cats rarely *meow* at each other. Meows are used mostly for grabbing the attention of humans!

If you want to smile at a cat, try narrowing your eyes and blinking very slowly. Cats make this facial expression when they are relaxed and content. Researchers in England have discovered that cats respond when humans do the same.

The Horse

A group of researchers in Norway trained horses to tell humans if they wanted to wear a blanket. The horses would touch symbols on a board, with their muzzle, to show if they would like the warm covering on or off. Their choices matched the weather.

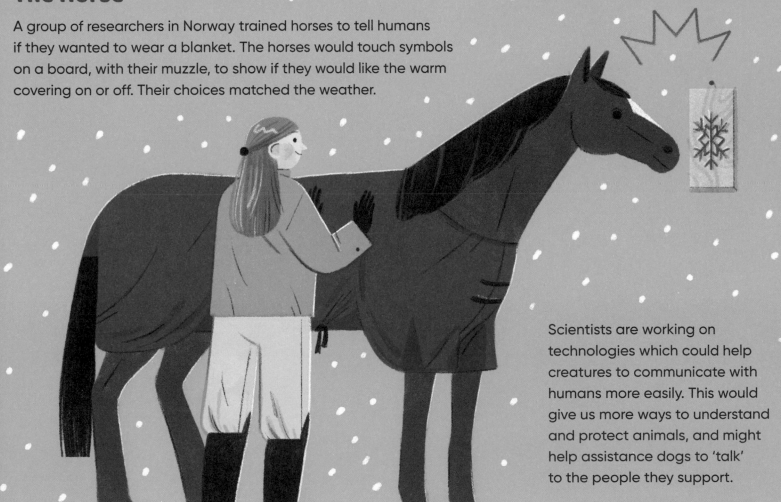

Scientists are working on technologies which could help creatures to communicate with humans more easily. This would give us more ways to understand and protect animals, and might help assistance dogs to 'talk' to the people they support.

Creatures have been 'talking' together here on Earth for millions of years – since long before humans walked the planet.

By watching and listening to the signals they send, we learn what animals want and need and even how they may be feeling.

When we understand what animals are saying,
we empathise with them and discover all the wonderful
ways in which we are connected. We are reminded
to protect them and treat them with respect.

And this works with our fellow human animals too.